SWEDEN

BY AMY RECHNER

BELLWETHER MEDIA • MINNEAPOLIS, MN

BLASTOFF!
DISCOVERY

Blastoff! Discovery launches a new mission: reading to learn. Filled with facts and features, each book offers you an exciting new world to explore!

This edition first published in 2018 by Bellwether Media, Inc.

Library of Congress Cataloging-in-Publication Data

Names: Rechner, Amy, author.
Title: Sweden / by Amy Rechner.
Description: Minneapolis, MN : Bellwether Media, Inc., 2018. |
    Series: Blastoff! Discovery: Country Profiles | Includes bibliographical
    references and index. | Audience: Age: 7-13.
Identifiers: LCCN 2017031937 (print) | LCCN 2017032981 (ebook)
    | ISBN 9781626177352 (hardcover : alk. paper) | ISBN
    9781681034898 (ebook)
Subjects: LCSH: Sweden–Juvenile literature.
Classification: LCC DL609 (ebook) | LCC DL609 .R43 2018 (print) |
    DDC 948.5–dc23
LC record available at https://lccn.loc.gov/2017031937

Editor: Paige V. Polinsky   Designer: Brittany McIntosh

Printed in the United States of America, North Mankato, MN.

TABLE OF CONTENTS

The early summer sun greets a visiting family in Stockholm. Their first stop is Skansen, an outdoor museum. Visitors go back in time as they wander through **traditional** Swedish settlements. A zoo and aquarium offer glimpses of Swedish wildlife.

STOCKHOLM

OTHER TOP SITES

DROTTNINGHOLM PALACE

ICEHOTEL, JUKKASJÄRVI

VIKING CITY OF BIRKA

VISBY, ISLAND OF GOTLAND

Next, they visit the Vasa Museum. A real 17th-century warship looms tall for everyone to view up close from the museum's six floors. There are **artifacts** and even skeletons from the wreck to marvel at. After dinner in a café, the family enjoys a sunny boat ride along Stockholm's canals before bed. This is Sweden!

Sweden covers 173,860 square miles (450,295 square kilometers) of a region called **Scandinavia**. It is one of the northernmost countries in Europe. Its northern region, called Lapland, lies partly in the **Arctic Circle**.

Sweden and its western neighbor, Norway, are on a **peninsula** that juts southwest from Finland. Along Sweden's eastern shore is the **Gulf** of Bothnia, which opens into the Baltic Sea. Stockholm, Sweden's capital, lies along the sea's coast. Denmark is off Sweden's southwestern shore, separated by narrow ocean **straits**. One is called the *Kattegat*, or "Cat's Throat." It connects the Baltic Sea to the North Sea.

NORWEGIAN SEA

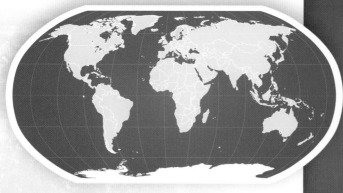

NORTH SEA

HERE COMES THE SUN

Because it is so far north, Stockholm has 18 hours of light in the summer, but only about 6 hours in the winter. Lapland winters may not have any light at all!

ARCTIC CIRCLE

SWEDEN

NORWAY

GULF OF BOTHNIA

FINLAND

UPPSALA - - - ●

STOCKHOLM - - - ★

● - - - GOTHENBURG

KATTEGAT

DENMARK

MALMÖ

BALTIC SEA

Sweden's northern **terrain** is covered with hills and forests. There, the country's highest peak, Mount Kebnekaise, stands 6,926 feet (2,111 meters) tall. It is part of the Scandinavian Mountains separating Sweden from Norway. The Torne and Muonio Rivers form the border with Finland. Central Sweden is covered with lakes, **plains**, and hills. A southern area called Skåne has excellent land for farming.

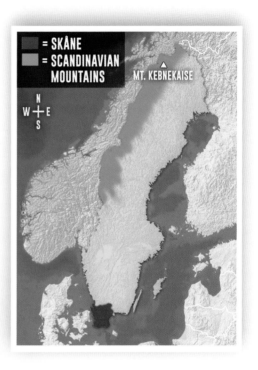

= SKÅNE
= SCANDINAVIAN MOUNTAINS
MT. KEBNEKAISE
N
W + E
S

LIGHT SHOW

The Northern Lights shine in dark skies in late fall and winter. Sweden's northern countryside is one of the best places to view them. Brilliant blue, pink, green, and purple lights sweep brightly across the sky.

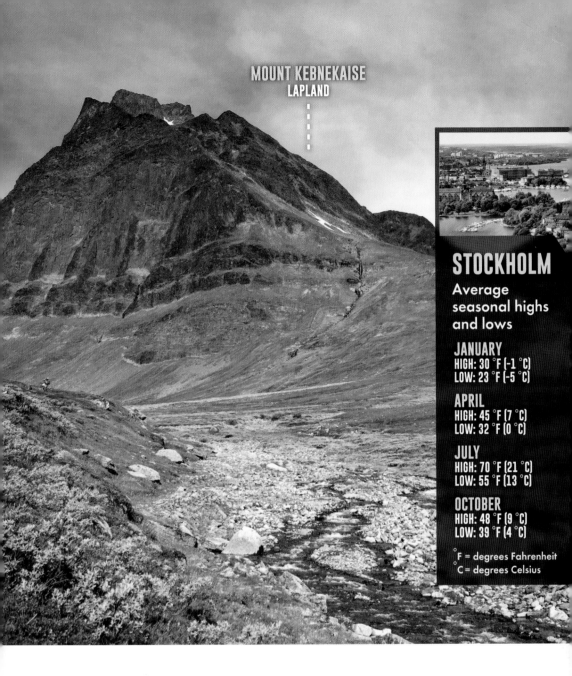

MOUNT KEBNEKAISE
LAPLAND

STOCKHOLM
Average
seasonal highs
and lows

JANUARY
HIGH: 30 °F (-1 °C)
LOW: 23 °F (-5 °C)

APRIL
HIGH: 45 °F (7 °C)
LOW: 32 °F (0 °C)

JULY
HIGH: 70 °F (21 °C)
LOW: 55 °F (13 °C)

OCTOBER
HIGH: 48 °F (9 °C)
LOW: 39 °F (4 °C)

°F = degrees Fahrenheit
°C = degrees Celsius

Because of the country's length, Sweden's climate varies. Northern Lapland is freezing cold and snowy in winters and cool in summers. Southern Sweden is more **temperate**. Summers are mild, and winters are cold with less snow.

WILDLIFE

Sweden is home to a wide range of wildlife. Moose, the national animal, live in forests and wooded areas throughout Sweden, along with bears. Arctic foxes stay in the northern mountains, where wolverines **scavenge** for food. In central Sweden, gray wolves and lynx prowl for prey, while beavers glide along rivers. Wild boars graze through the fields and woods of the southern region.

Sweden's many lakes and rivers are home to salmon, pike, trout, and perch. Gray seals live off the rocky coasts. **Habitats** like tree-lined **marshes** attract owls, ospreys, and woodpeckers.

GRAY WOLF

OSPREY

BROWN BEAR

WOLVERINE

BEARS WITH BLUE TEETH

In Sweden, bears are wild for blueberries! One bear can eat around 180,000 blueberries in a single day.

MOOSE

MOOSE
(EUROPEAN ELK)

Life Span: 15-20 years
Red List Status: least concern

moose range =

LEAST CONCERN	NEAR THREATENED	VULNERABLE	ENDANGERED	CRITICALLY ENDANGERED	EXTINCT IN THE WILD	EXTINCT

REINDEER TRACKS

The Sami people have lived for more than two thousand years in the Laplands of Norway, Finland, northwestern Russia, and Sweden. Many still fish and tend herds of reindeer in the frozen north. Others live modern lives and hold regular jobs.

Most of the nearly 10 million people who live in Sweden are Swedish. Many Finns live there, too. Other people **emigrated** from **Middle Eastern** countries like Syria and Iraq. The majority of residents live in **urban** areas in the south. A **native** group called the Sami lives in Lapland. Although the official language is Swedish, communities including the Sami and Finns speak their own languages, too.

Many Swedes belong to the Christian Lutheran Church of Sweden. Other Swedes are different kinds of Christians. Some people are Muslim, Jewish, or Buddhist. Most Swedes go to church only on religious holidays. Some do not follow any religion.

FAMOUS FACE

Name: **Daniel Ek**
Birthday: **February 21, 1983**
Hometown: **Stockholm, Sweden**
Famous for: **Co-founder and CEO of Spotify, the Internet music-streaming service that allows users to listen to millions of songs through the Spotify app**

SPEAK SWEDISH

ENGLISH	SWEDISH	HOW TO SAY IT
hello	hej	hey
goodbye	hej då	hey DOH
please	tack	tahck
thank you	tack	tahck
yes	ja	yaw
no	nej	nay

STOCKHOLM

Rural Sweden is known for its red houses. Urban Swedes live in apartments and houses. Most Swedish families own a car. However, they usually use the many options for public transportation instead, such as railways and buses. They also bicycle or walk to get around. These methods help prevent pollution. Sweden is very careful to preserve the environment for future communities.

STOCKHOLM

DON'T FENCE ME IN

Hikers, berry pickers, and mushroom hunters can go wherever they want in Sweden. As long as they avoid private areas and do not get too close to houses, people can wander across property lines. Everyone is expected to treat the land with respect.

The Swedish people are very independent. Grandparents usually live on their own instead of with family. Families are small, with only one or two children. Women and men share equal roles in society, so usually both parents work.

THE GOLDILOCKS LIFE

The Swedish way of life is summed up in the word *lagom*. It means, "not too much, not too little, just enough." Among other things, this simple idea affects behavior, food choices, and conversation.

CHOKLADKOPPEN

Swedes do not call attention to themselves or get too competitive. It is part of their *lagom* way of life. They are polite but **reserved**. They do not like their personal space invaded and avoid standing or sitting too close to others.

However, Swedes cherish time with family and friends. Every day they take a break for *fika*, a time for coffee and pastries. It is more common to invite friends over for fika than for dinner. Visitors are expected to be on time and to take off their shoes when they enter.

FIKA

Students in Sweden begin school at age 7. Most attend at
least one year of preschool first. Students must attend school
until age 16. As they move past required education, they
can prepare for university or train for different jobs. About
half attend one of the country's many universities.

Most of the workers in Sweden have jobs in services like health care, education, or government. Swedish technology companies like Spotify and Mojang employ many workers. Furniture giant IKEA also employs Swedes to design its products. Other people **manufacture** products like automobiles or paper products. A small number of farmers raise livestock.

IKEA WORKER

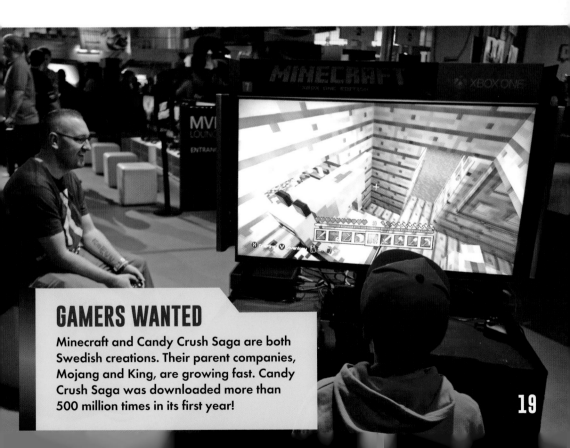

GAMERS WANTED

Minecraft and Candy Crush Saga are both Swedish creations. Their parent companies, Mojang and King, are growing fast. Candy Crush Saga was downloaded more than 500 million times in its first year!

19

BERRY PICKING

Spending time enjoying the outdoors is very important to Swedes. Many urban families own or rent country cottages. They spend long summer days picking berries. They also go hiking, fishing, swimming, or boating. In winter, they enjoy skiing and ice skating.

HOCKEY

Organized sports like hockey are also a part of Swedish life. Soccer, which they call football, is very popular with children as well as adults. Sweden has produced many world-class tennis players. Swedes also enjoy a rich tradition of film, books, plays, and music. Swedish children learn to play instruments at an early age.

TENNIS

KUBB

Kubb, pronounced koob, is an outdoor game also known as Viking chess. Play it in an open green space with two to twelve players.

What You Need:
- 10 12-ounce plastic bottles, filled partway with water – the kubbs
- 1 2-liter plastic bottle, filled partway with water – the King
- 6 wooden spoons or spatulas – the batons

How to Play:
1. Place five kubbs in a line, about 1 foot (30 centimeters) apart. Walk twenty steps and place the other five kubbs in a line, across from the others. Put the King in the middle of the two lines.
2. Team 1 takes the batons and throws their batons underhand across the field at the kubbs. After all batons have been thrown, Team 2 throws any knocked over kubbs into Team 1's part of the field. Team 1 stands them up in the field as field kubbs.
3. Now it is Team 2's turn. They must knock the field kubbs over before they can hit Team 1's kubbs.
4. When a team has knocked over all of the opposing team's kubbs, they can try to hit the King. The first team to knock down the King wins. If the King is knocked over early, the team that hit him loses.

TASTE OF SUMMER

The August crayfish party is a favorite celebration. Family and friends gather outside around a table heaped with boiled crayfish. Everyone wears paper hats and bibs. Then they bid farewell to summer by eating crayfish, bread, and cheese with their fingers.

Sweden's foods follow the seasons. Nettle soup is common in spring. Fish and fruit are eaten fresh in the warmer months and preserved for winter. Salmon is cured and turned into *gravlax*. Small fish called herring are pickled. Blueberries, cloudberries, and lingonberries are made into jams and syrups. Root vegetables like potatoes and beets are winter **staples**.

Breakfast is small, usually just bread and yogurt or porridge. Lunch is eaten at work or school. Dinner is the big meal of the day. Meatballs are a favorite meal. Pea soup and pancakes for Thursday dinner is a Swedish tradition. Celebrations bring long buffet tables called *smorgasbords* filled with food.

NETTLE SOUP

GRAVLAX

KLADDKAKA (STICKY CAKE) RECIPE

This brownie-like Swedish treat is easy to make and a popular fika treat. Ask an adult to help with the oven.

Ingredients:
3/4 cup (1/2 stick) butter
1 1/2 cup sugar
1/2 cup unsweetened cocoa
2 teaspoons vanilla extract
2 eggs
1 cup flour
cooking spray

Steps:
1. Preheat oven to 400 degrees Fahrenheit (204 degrees Celsius).
2. Put the butter in a medium-sized, microwave-safe bowl. Microwave on high power for about 1 minute, or until butter is melted. Let cool.
3. While butter is cooling, spray cooking spray into an 8-inch pie plate or square baking pan.
4. Add other ingredients to butter, stirring after each one. Add flour last. Stir well.
5. Pour the batter into the pan, using a spatula to scrape the sides of the bowl.
6. Bake for 18-20 minutes.
7. Let cool. Cut into pieces and serve with whipped cream or ice cream.

MIDSUMMER

Sweden finds joy in changing seasons. At Easter time, children dress as witches and trade homemade crafts for treats. April 30 is Walpurgis Eve. Swedes sing songs around bonfires to welcome spring. Midsummer celebrates the arrival of summer. Children make flower wreaths and dance around the **maypole**. Many people wear traditional clothes.

December 13 is St. Lucia Day. In towns all over Sweden, a girl dressed as Saint Lucia wears a wreath crown with lit candles. She leads children wearing white and carrying candles through the snowy streets. They sing and give away special pastries. The candles and music highlight the beauty of Sweden!

ST. LUCIA DAY

1397
Queen Margaret of Sweden installs her nephew, Erik, as ruler of Denmark, Sweden, and Norway

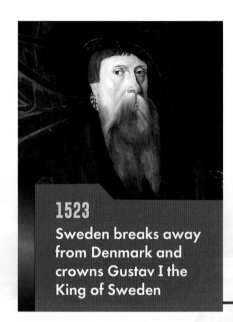

1523
Sweden breaks away from Denmark and crowns Gustav I the King of Sweden

550 CE
After many years of unrest, Sweden becomes a settled society that relies on farming

800
The people of Sweden, known as Vikings, begin their attacks on Eastern Europe

1630
Sweden joins the Thirty Years War and later wins control of several German territories

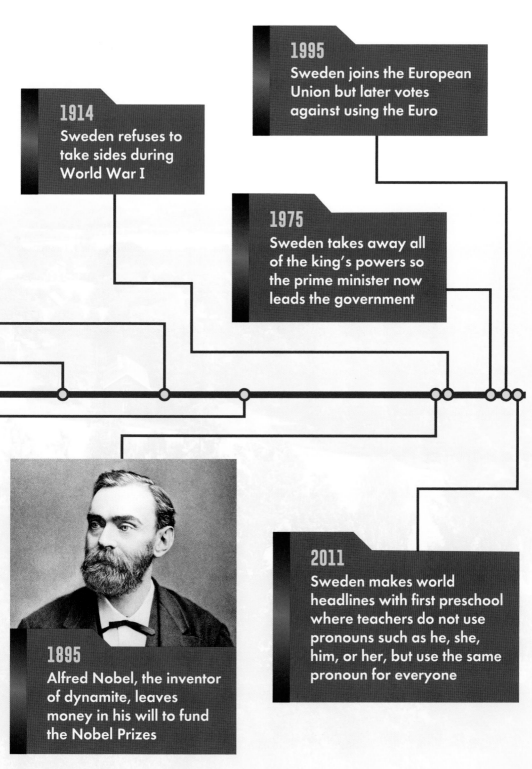

1995
Sweden joins the European Union but later votes against using the Euro

1914
Sweden refuses to take sides during World War I

1975
Sweden takes away all of the king's powers so the prime minister now leads the government

2011
Sweden makes world headlines with first preschool where teachers do not use pronouns such as he, she, him, or her, but use the same pronoun for everyone

1895
Alfred Nobel, the inventor of dynamite, leaves money in his will to fund the Nobel Prizes

27

Official Name: Kingdom of Sweden

Flag of Sweden: Sweden's flag is blue with a golden yellow cross that reaches the end of the flag, known as the Nordic Cross. The upright arm of the cross is to the left of center.

Area: 173,860 square miles
(450,295 square kilometers)

Capital City: Stockholm

Important Cities: Gothenburg,
Malmö, Uppsala

Population:
9,960,487 (July 2017)

WHERE
PEOPLE LIVE

COUNTRYSIDE
13.9%

CITY
86.1%

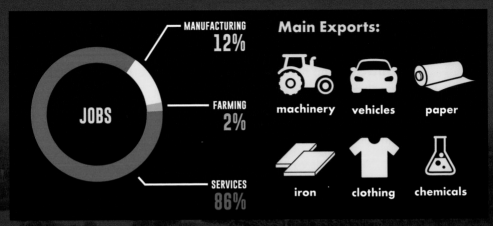

MANUFACTURING
12%

JOBS

FARMING
2%

SERVICES
86%

Main Exports:

machinery

vehicles

paper

iron

clothing

chemicals

National Holiday:
National Day (June 6)

Main Language:
Swedish

Form of Government:
parliamentary constitutional monarchy

Title for Country Leaders:
king, prime minister

RELIGION

NONE
20%

OTHER
17%

LUTHERAN
63%

Unit of Money:
krona

GLOSSARY

Arctic Circle—an imaginary line that circles the top of the globe, parallel to the equator

artifacts—items made long ago by humans; artifacts tell people today about people from the past.

emigrated—left a country or region to move to another country

gulf—part of an ocean or sea that extends into land

habitats—lands with certain types of plants, animals, and weather

manufacture—to make products, often with machines

marshes—wetlands that are filled with grasses

maypole—a tall pole decorated with ribbons and flowers

Middle Eastern—from a region of southwestern Asia and northern Africa; this region includes Egypt, Lebanon, Iran, Iraq, Israel, Saudi Arabia, Syria, and other nearby countries.

native—originally from the area or related to a group of people that began in the area

peninsula—a section of land that extends out from a larger piece of land and is almost completely surrounded by water

plains—large areas of flat land

reserved—cautious in words and actions

rural—related to the countryside

Scandinavia—a region of northern Europe that includes Sweden, Denmark, and Norway

scavenge—to look for food that is already dead

staples—widely used foods or other items

straits—narrow channels connecting two large bodies of water

temperate—associated with a mild climate that does not have extreme heat or cold

terrain—the surface features of an area of land

traditional—related to customs, ideas, or beliefs handed down from one generation to the next

urban—related to cities and city life

TO LEARN MORE

AT THE LIBRARY

Hyde, Natalie. *Cultural Traditions in Sweden.* St. Catharines, Ont.: Crabtree Publishing Company, 2015.

Kemper, Bitsy. *Sweden.* Mankato, Minn.: Child's World, 2015.

Shea, Therese. *Vikings.* New York, N.Y.: Britannica Educational Publishing, 2016.

ON THE WEB

Learning more about Sweden is as easy as 1, 2, 3.

1. Go to www.factsurfer.com.

2. Enter "Sweden" into the search box.

3. Click the "Surf" button and you will see a list of related web sites.

With factsurfer.com, finding more information is just a click away.

INDEX